BACKYARD WILDLIFE

Mountain Lions

by Kristin Schuetz

BELLWETHER MEDIA • MINNEAPOLIS, MN

Note to Librarians, Teachers, and Parents:

Blastoff! Readers are carefully developed by literacy experts and combine standards-based content with developmentally appropriate text.

Level 1 provides the most support through repetition of high-frequency words, light text, predictable sentence patterns, and strong visual support.

Level 2 offers early readers a bit more challenge through varied simple sentences, increased text load, and less repetition of high-frequency words.

Level 3 advances early-fluent readers toward fluency through increased text and concept load, less reliance on visuals, longer sentences, and more literary language.

Level 4 builds reading stamina by providing more text per page, increased use of punctuation, greater variation in sentence patterns, and increasingly challenging vocabulary.

Level 5 encourages children to move from "learning to read" to "reading to learn" by providing even more text, varied writing styles, and less familiar topics.

Whichever book is right for your reader, Blastoff! Readers are the perfect books to build confidence and encourage a love of reading that will last a lifetime!

This edition first published in 2014 by Bellwether Media, Inc.

No part of this publication may be reproduced in whole or in part without written permission of the publisher. For information regarding permission, write to Bellwether Media, Inc., Attention: Permissions Department, 5357 Penn Avenue South, Minneapolis, MN 55419.

Library of Congress Cataloging-in-Publication Data

Schuetz, Kristin, author.
  Mountain Lions / by Kristin Schuetz.
    pages cm. – (Blastoff! Readers. Backyard Wildlife)
  Summary: "Developed by literacy experts for students in kindergarten through grade three, this book introduces mountain lions to young readers through leveled text and related photos"– Provided by publisher.
  Audience: Age 5-8.
  Audience: Grades K to 3.
  Includes bibliographical references and index.
  ISBN 978-1-60014-970-2 (hardcover : alk. paper)
  1. Puma–Juvenile literature. I. Title. II. Series: Blastoff! readers. 1, Backyard wildlife.
  QL737.C23S346 2014
  599.75'24–dc23
                                                                    2014000821

Contents

Mountain lions are **mammals** that have many names. They are also called cougars and pumas.

These **wild cats** have strong legs. They can run fast and jump far.

Mountain lions live alone in forests, **prairies**, and deserts.

They rest in
bushes and
rocky areas
during the day.

Mountain lions hunt at night. They **stalk** rabbits, deer, and other **prey**.

They **ambush** animals with a powerful **pounce**. A bite to the neck kills.

Then mountain lions feast. They hide leftovers under leaves and branches for later.

Mothers give birth to one to six **cubs**. The cubs have blue eyes and spotted bodies.

Cubs hide when mom hunts. Their spots **camouflage** them. Stay out of sight!

Glossary

ambush—to attack something or someone by surprise

camouflage—to help something blend in with the surroundings

cubs—young mountain lions

mammals—warm-blooded animals that have backbones and feed milk to their young

pounce—to leap on top of something

prairies—large areas of flat grassland with few trees

prey—animals that are hunted by other animals for food

stalk—to secretly follow

wild cats—cats that live in nature

To Learn More

AT THE LIBRARY

Magby, Meryl. *Mountain Lions*. New York, N.Y.: PowerKids Press, 2014.

Raatma, Lucia. *Mountain Lions*. Ann Arbor, Mich.: Cherry Lake Pub., 2010.

Randall, Henry. *Cougars*. New York, N.Y.: PowerKids Press, 2011.

ON THE WEB

Learning more about mountain lions is as easy as 1, 2, 3.

1. Go to www.factsurfer.com.

2. Enter "mountain lions" into the search box.

3. Click the "Surf" button and you will see a list of related web sites.

With factsurfer.com, finding more information is just a click away.

Index